Yellowstone National Park: The History

By Charles River Editors

Old Faithful

About Charles River Editors

Charles River Editors provides superior editing and original writing services across the digital publishing industry, with the expertise to create digital content for publishers across a vast range of subject matter. In addition to providing original digital content for third party publishers, we also republish civilization's greatest literary works, bringing them to new generations of readers via ebooks.

Sign up here to receive updates about free books as we publish them, and visit Our Kindle Author Page to browse today's free promotions and our most recently published Kindle titles.

Introduction

Castle Geyser

Yellowstone National Park

"Judge, then, what must have been our astonishment, as we entered the basin at mid-afternoon of our second day's travel, to see in the clear sunlight, at no great distance, an immense volume of clear, sparkling water projected into the air to the height of one hundred and twenty-five feet. "Geysers! geysers!" exclaimed one of our company, and, spurring our jaded horses, we soon gathered around this wonderful phenomenon. It was indeed a perfect geyser. The aperture through which the jet was projected was an irregular oval, three feet by seven in diameter. The margin of sinter was curiously piled up, and the exterior crust was filled with little hollows full of water, in which were small globules of sediment, some having gathered around bits of wood and other nuclei. This geyser is elevated thirty feet above the level of the surrounding plain, and the crater rises five or six feet above the mound. It spouted at regular intervals nine times during our stay, the columns of boiling water being thrown from ninety to one hundred and twenty-five feet at each discharge, which lasted from fifteen to twenty minutes. We gave it the name of 'Old Faithful.'" – Nathaniel P. Langford

The United States is full of natural wonders, but few rival Yellowstone National Park, which is full of features that led Native Americans to believe the land was possessed by spirits and compelled people who heard accounts from white explorers to assume the explorers had suffered hallucinations. Today, of course, all Americans are instantly familiar with the name Old Faithful, and even among those who have never visited the park, Yellowstone is practically synonymous with its geysers.

While Old Faithful and other geysers remain the park's most popular features, Yellowstone offers a vast array of diversity, not only among wildlife but within the land itself. Yellowstone is home to mountains, rivers, canyons, lakes, forests, waterfalls, and North America's largest supervolcano, which remains active underneath Yellowstone Lake. While all of this attracts millions of tourists, Yellowstone is also home to all kinds of animals, from bison to birds, some of which are endangered species protected within the park. Established by President Ulysses S. Grant, Yellowstone is one of America's most ambitious and crucial conservation areas, and nearly 150 years later, officials still try to balance the interests of everyone and everything involved.

Yellowstone National Park: The History of America's Most Famous Park traces the history of the park's establishment and historic descriptions of its features. Along with pictures of important people, places, and events, you will learn about Yellowstone like never before, in no time at all.

Yellowstone National Park: The History of America's Most Famous Park
About Charles River Editors
Introduction
    Chapter 1: Pure Sulphur is Sent Forth
    Chapter 2: A Branch of the Yellow Stone
    Chapter 3: A Large Basin
    Chapter 4: These Greatest Falls
    Chapter 5: A Park Worthy of the Great Republic
    Bibliography

Chapter 1: Pure Sulphur is Sent Forth

Daniel Mayer's picture of Bunsen Peak

"At or near this place heads the Luchkadee or Californ [Green River] Stinking Fork [Shoshone River] Yellow-Stone South fork of Masuri and Henrys Fork all those head at an angular point. That of the Yellow-Stone has a large fresh water Lake near its head on the very top of the Mountain, which is about one hundred by forty Miles in diameter and as clear as Crystal. On the South borders of this Lake is a number of hot and boiling springs, some of water and others of most beautiful fine clay and resembles that of a mush pot and throws its particles to the immense height of from twenty to thirty feet in height. The Clay is white and of a pink and water appears fathomless as it appears to be entirely hollow underneath. There is also a number of places where the pure sulphur is sent forth in abundance. "One of our men visited one of those whilst taking his recreation there at an instant the earth began a tremendous trembling and he with difficulty made his escape, when an explosion took place resembling that of thunder. During our stay in that quarter I heard it every day." - Fur-trapper Daniel Potts, writing to his brother in the 1820s

Before there was a Yellowstone National Park, or any other national park for that matter, there was the Yellowstone River and the land that surrounded it. Though they travelled along the Yellowstone River, from which the park gets its name, Lewis and Clark just missed the important features of the land at the corner of what is now Montana and Wyoming. Instead, they merely noted, "At the head of this river the natives give an account that there is frequently heard a loud noise, like Thunder, which makes the earth Tremble, they State that they seldom go there because their children Cannot sleep—and Conceive it possessed of spirits, who were averse that men Should be near them." Later, one of their fellow explorers, John Colter, returned to explore the area in depth. When he later told the story of streams of boiling water that shot up out of the ground, those hearing him speak assumed he was hallucinating and had perhaps caught some sort of fever during his wanderings.

Lewis and Clark

A few years later, in 1829, 19 year old Joseph Meek made a frightening acquaintance with the park's most famous features. Eventually, he told what seems to be (at least according to Yellowstone experts) a somewhat exaggerated story to a neighbor, who later repeated how Meek "ascended a low mountain in the neighborhood of his camp—and behold! the whole country beyond was smoking with the vapor from boiling springs, and burning with gasses, issuing from small' craters, each of which was emitting a sharp whistling sound. When the first surprise of this astonishing scene had passed, Joe began to ad mire its effect in an artistic point of view. The morning being clear, with a sharp frost, he thought himself reminded of the city of Pittsburg, as he had beheld it on a winter morning a couple of years before. This, however, related only to the rising smoke and vapor; for the extent of the volcanic region was immense, reaching far out of sight. The general face of the country was smooth and rolling, being a level plain, dotted with cone-shaped mounds. On the summits of these mounds were small craters from four to eight feet in diameter. Interspersed among these, on the level plain, were larger craters, some of them from four to six miles across. Out of these craters issued blue flames and molten brimstone. For some minutes Joe gazed and wondered. Curious thoughts came into his head, about hell and the day of doom. With that natural tendency to reckless gayety and humorous absurdities which some temperaments are sensible of in times of great excitement, he began to soliloquize. Said he, to himself, 'I have been told the sun would be blown out, and the earth burnt up. If this infernal wind keeps up, I shouldn't be surprised if the sun [was] blown out. If the earth is not burning up over thar, then it is that place the old Methodist preacher used to threaten me with. Any way it suits me to go and see what it's like.' On descending to the plain described, the earth was found to have a hollow sound, and seemed threatening to break through. But Joe found the warmth of the place most delightful, after the freezing cold of the mountains, and remarked to himself again, that 'if it [was] hell, it [was] a more agreeable climate than he had been in for some time."

In 1833, Manuel Alvarez became the first recorded individual to visit Yellowstone for no other reason than that it was there, and as a result, some consider him Yellowstone's first tourist. He wrote of his adventure at the Firehole River Basins, "We proceeded over the plain about twenty miles, and halted until day-light, on a fine spring, flowing into Cammas Creek. Refreshed by a few hours sleep, we started again after a hasty breakfast, and entered a very extensive forest, called the Piny Woods; (a continuous succession of low mountains or hills, entirely covered by a dense growth of this species of timber;) which we passed through, and reached the vicinity of the springs about dark, having seen several small lakes or ponds on the sources of the Madison, and rode about forty miles…When I arose in the morning, clouds of vapor seemed like a dense fog to overhang the springs, from which frequent reports or explosions of different loudness, constantly assailed our ears. I immediately proceeded to inspect them…From the surface of a rocky plain or table, burst forth columns of water of various dimensions, projected high in the air, accompanied by loud explosions, and sulphurous vapors, which were highly disagreeable to the smell. The rock from which these springs burst forth, was calcareous, and probably extends some distance from them, beneath the soil. The largest of these wonderful fountains, projects a column of boiling water several feet in diameter, to the height of more than one hundred and fifty feet, in my opinion…These explosions and discharges occur at intervals of about two hours. After having witnessed three of them, I ventured near enough to put my hand into the water of its basin, but withdrew it instantly, for the heat of the water in this immense cauldron, was altogether too great for my comfort; and the agitation of the water, the disagreeable effluvium continually exuding, and the hollow unearthly rumbling under the rock on which I stood, so ill accorded with my notions of personal safety, that I retreated back precipitately, to a respectful distance."

Brocken Inaglory's picture of a geyser at Firehole River

A picture of water runoff from Excelsior Geyser to Firehole River

Having dispensed with the tale of his own curiosity and perhaps even foolishness, Alvarez proceeded to describe the water within it natural surroundings: "The diameter of the basin into which the waters of the largest jet principally fall, and from the center of which, through a hole in the rock of about nine or ten feet in diameter, the water spouts up as above related, may be about thirty feet. There are many other smaller fountains, that did not throw their water up so high, but occurred at shorter intervals. In some instances the volumes were projected obliquely upwards, and fell into the neighboring fountains, or on the rock or prairie. But their ascent was generally perpendicular, falling in and about their own basins or apertures. These wonderful productions of nature, are situated near the center of a small valley, surrounded by pine-crowned hills, through which a small fork of the Madison flows."

Alvarez next went on to describe a section of the area that was likely the same one earlier called "Bee Hive": "From several trappers who had recently returned from the Yellow Stone, I received an account of boiling springs, that differ from those seen on Salt River only in magnitude, being on a vastly larger scale; some of their cones are from twenty to thirty feet high, and forty to fifty paces in circumference. Those which have ceased to emit boiling, vapor, etc., of which there were several, are full of shelving cavities, even some fathoms in extent, which give them, inside, an appearance of honey-comb. The ground for several acres extent in vicinity of the springs is evidently hollow, and constantly exhales a hot steam or vapor of disagreeable odor, and a character entirely to prevent vegetation. They are situated in the valley at the head of that river, near the lake, which constitutes its source."

Picture of Beehive Geyser erupting

Alvarez's final observation is perhaps the strangest, for explorers and scientists have never been able to determine the exact place he was talking about. Still, those in the know believe him to have been honest in his observations, since there were several similar lakes in the park to this day. "A short distance from these springs, near the margin of the lake, there is one quite different from any yet described. It is of a circular form, several feet in diameter, clear, cold and pure; the bottom appears visible to the eye and seems seven or eight feet below the surface of the earth or water, yet it has been sounded with a lodge pole fifteen feet in length, without meeting any resistance. What is most singular with respect to this fountain, is the fact that at regular intervals of about two minutes, a body or column of water bursts up to the height of eight feet, with an explosion as loud as the report of [a] musket, and then falls back into it; for a few seconds the water is roily, but it speedily settles, and becomes transparent as before the effluxion. A slight tremulous motion of the water and a low rumbling sound from the caverns beneath, precede each explosion. This spring was believed to be connected with the lake by some subterranean passage, but the cause of its periodical eruptions or discharges, is entirely unknown. I have never before heard of a cold spring, whose waters exhibit the phenomena of periodical explosive propulsion, in form of a jet. The geysers of Iceland, and the various other European springs, the waters of which are projected upwards, with violence and uniformity, as well as those seen on the head waters of the Madison, are invariably hot."

Chapter 2: A Branch of the Yellow Stone

Daniel Mayer's picture of Gibbon Falls

Daniel Mayer's picture of Tower Falls

"We crossed the mountain in a West direction through the thick pines and fallen timber about 12 miles and encamped in a small prairie about a mile in circumference. Through this valley ran a small stream in a north direction which all agreed in believing to be a branch of the Yellow Stone. ... We descended the stream about 15 miles through the dense forest and at length came to a beautiful valley about 8 miles long and 3 or 4 wide surrounded by dark and lofty mountains. The stream after running through the center in a NW direction rushed down a tremendous canyon of basaltic rock apparently just wide enough to admit its waters. The banks of the stream in the valley were low and skirted in many places with beautiful Cotton wood groves. ... Our Geographer also told us that this stream united with the Yellow Stone after leaving this Valley half a day's travel in a west direction. The river then ran a long distance through a tremendous cut in the mountain in the same direction and emerged into a large plain the extent of which was beyond his geographical knowledge or conception." - Osborne Russell

While the geysers were and remain the most dramatic feature in what is now Yellowstone National Park, they are far from the only objects of natural beauty in the area. In some cases, they snuck up on 18th century Americans, as was the case with Osborne Russell, who had no particular interest in seeing new sites when he wondered into the Yellowstone region in July 1835. Russell was simply looking for a new site to ply his trade as a trapper, and he wrote an account of the area after seeing it again in August 1836: "[W]e came to a smooth prairie about 2 Miles long and half a Mile wide lying east and west surrounded by pines. On the South side about midway of the prairie stands a high snowy peak from whence issues a Stream of water which after entering the plain it divides equally one half running West and the other East thus bidding adieu to each other one bound for the Pacific and the other for the Atlantic ocean. Here a trout of 12 inches in length may cross the mountains in safety. ... The [Yellowstone] Lake is about 100 Miles in circumference bordered on the East by high ranges of Mountains whose spurs terminate at the shore and on the west by a low bed of piney mountains its greatest width is about 15 Miles lying in an oblong form south to north or rather in the shape of a crescent. Near where we encamped were several hot springs which boil perpetually. Near these was an opening in the ground about 8 inches in diameter from which steam issues continually with a noise similar to that made by the steam issuing from a safety valve of an engine and can be heard 5 or 6 Miles distant. I should think the steam issued with sufficient force to work an engine of 30 horse power."

Yellowstone Lake

A geyser at Yellowstone Lake

The supervolcano jutting out of Yellowstone Lake

Finally, in 1839, Russell found himself in the presence of the great geysers themselves. He wrote, "The first thing that attracts the attention is a hole about 15 inches in diameter in which the water is boiling slowly about 4 inches below the surface at length it begins to boil and bubble violently and the water commences raising and shooting upwards until the column arises to the height of sixty feet from whence it falls to the ground in drops on a circle of about 30 feet in diameter being perfectly cold when it strikes the ground. It continues shooting up in this manner five or six minutes and then sinks back to its former state of Slowly boiling for an hour and then shoots forth as before. My Comrade Said he had watched the motions of this Spring for one whole day and part of the night the year previous and found no irregularity whatever in its movements."

Russell soon became the first man to record a strange, "patriotic" phenomenon in one of the Yellowstone streams, and there are similar scenes in the park today: "At length we came to a boiling Lake about 300 feet in diameter forming nearly a complete circle as we approached on the South side. The steam which arose from it was of three distinct Colors from the west side for one third of the diameter it was white, in the middle it was pale red, and the remaining third on the east light sky blue. Whether it was something peculiar in the state of the atmosphere the day being cloudy or whether it was some Chemical properties contained in the water which produced this phenomenon, I am unable to say and shall leave the explanation to some scientific tourist who may have the Curiosity to visit this place at some future period—The water was of deep indigo blue boiling like an immense cauldron running over the white rock which had formed [round] the edges to the height of 4 or 5 feet from the surface of the earth sloping gradually for 60 or 70 feet. What a field of speculation this presents for chemist and geologist."

Morning Glory Pool

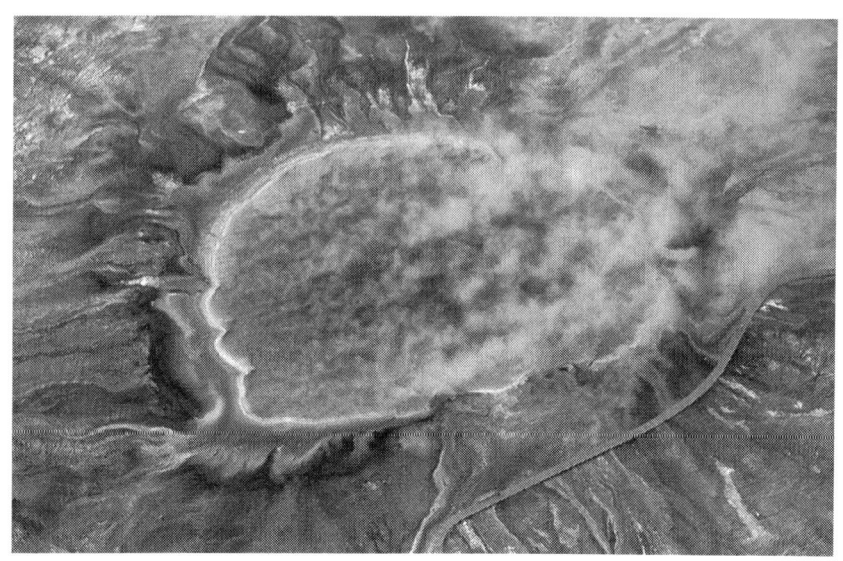

Grand Prismatic Spring

Surprise Pool

Within a decade or so of its discovery, the Yellowstone area began to attract visitors from other parts of the country and world. Most came to hunt, but many also wanted to see the strange phenomena they had heard about. In 1843, Sir William Drommond Stewart visited the region from Scotland, and a young man who was travelling with him later wrote that "we reached a country that seemed, indeed, to be Nature's wonderworld. The rugged grandeur of the landscape was most impressive, and the beauty of the crystal-clear water falling over huge rocks was a picture to carry forever in one's mind. Here was an ideal spot to camp; so we broke ranks and settled down to our first night's rest in the region now known as Yellowstone National Park. On approaching, we had noticed at regular intervals of about five or ten minutes what seemed to be a tall column of smoke or steam, such as would arise from a steamboat. On nearer approach, however, we discovered it to be a geyser, which we christened 'Steam Boat Geyser.' Several other geysers were found nearby, some of them so hot that we boiled our bacon in them.... One geyser, a soda spring, was so effervescent that I believe the syrup to be the only thing lacking to make it equal a giant ice cream soda of the kind now popular at a drugstore."

Still, it remained for the renowned explorer and frontiersman Jim Bridger to offer the description of the land that would truly catch the nation's imagination. In 1852, Lt. John W. Gunnison wrote of what Bridger had told him: "He gives a picture, most romantic and enticing, of the headwaters of the Yellowstone. A lake, sixty miles long, cold and pellucid, lies embosomed among high precipitous mountains. On the westside is a sloping plain, several miles wide, with clumps of trees and groves of pine. The ground resounds with the tread of horses. Geysers spout up seventy feet high, with a terrific, hissing noise, at regular intervals. Waterfalls are sparkling, leaping and thundering down the precipices, and collect in the pool below. The river issues from this lake, and for fifteen miles roars through the perpendicular canyon at the outlet. In this section are the 'Great Springs,' so hot that meat is readily cooked in them, and as they descend on the successive terraces, afford at length delightful baths. On the other side is an acid spring, which gushes out in a river torrent; and below is a cave, which supplies 'vermilion' for the savages in abundance. Bear, elk, deer, wolf, and fox are among the game, and the feathered tribe yields its share for variety, on the sportsman's table of rock or turf."

Bridger

  By the late 1840s, efforts had begun to map the region that would, within a few short decades, be set aside for special protection by the federal government. In 1851, Bridger himself made a map of the area for a Jesuit priest, Father Pierre-Jean DeSmet, to aid him in his missionary work among the Native Americans in the area. Over time, DeSmet made his own adjustments to the map based on his travels, and he later wrote of Yellowstone: "Near the source of the river Puante [Stinking Water, now called Shoshone] which empties into the Big Horn, and the sulphurous waters of which have probably the same medicinal qualities as the celebrated Blue Lick Springs of Kentucky, is a place called Colter's Hell—from a beaver hunter of that name. This locality is often agitated with subterranean fires. The sulphurous gases which escape in great volumes from the burning soil infect the atmosphere for several miles, and render the earth so barren that even the wild worm wood cannot grow on it. The beaver hunters have assured me that the frequent underground noises and explosions are frightful. However, I think that the most extraordinary spot in this respect, and perhaps the most marvelous of all the northern half of this continent, is in the very heart of the Rocky Mountains, between the forty-third and forty-fifth degrees of latitude and 109th and 11th degrees of longitude, that is, between the sources of the Madison and Yellowstone. It reaches more than a hundred miles. Bituminous, sulphurous and boiling springs are very numerous in it. The hot springs contain a large quantity of calcareous matter [silicious], and form hills more or less elevated, which resemble in their nature, perhaps, if not in their extent, the famous springs of Pambuk Kalessi, in Asia Minor...The earth is thrown up very high, and the influence of the elements causes it to take the most varied and the most fantastic shapes. Gas, vapor and smoke are continually escaping by a thousand openings, from the base to the summit of the volcanic pile; the noise at times resembles the steam let off by a boat. Strong subterranean explosions occur, like those in 'Colter's Hell'. The hunters and Indians speak of it with a superstitious fear, and consider it the abode of evil spirits, that is to say, a kind of hell."

Shoshone Lake

Chapter 3: A Large Basin

"We 'nooned' on the left bank of this stream, and then continued our way north, crossing the river again, by a deep ford, in about three miles, and camped for the evening on the edge of a small prairie, near where a large fork came in the southeast. On the left bank of the south fork was a high, perpendicular wall of rock, and we could see the smoke of hot springs up the east fork [Terrace Spring]. ...we were at the forks of the Fire Hole River, a branch of the Madison.

In the morning (September 10th), we continued our journey down the main river, crossing the east fork just above the junction. The weather looked stormy and threatening. The main river was about fifty yards wide, its valley very narrow, with high, rocky hills on either side covered with pine, and the general course westerly. … In the evening, during an interval of calm, I went forward on the trail across the mountain to explore. In about one and half miles I came to the foot of the cañon, when I perceived that the country opened out into a large basin, through which the main river ran." - Walter W. De Lacy

Like so many other facets of Western expansion, the exploration of Yellowstone was driven forward by the search for gold and other precious metals. In 1863, 40 prospectors organized themselves to explore the Snake River in their search for undiscovered riches. Their leader, Walter De Lacy, kept extensive notes about what he saw and later wrote of his adventures within the region of the Lower Geyser: "On starting, we kept a northerly course and passed over low undulating ridges, covered with open pine timber [Pitchstone Plateau]. The rocks, where exposed, seem to be vitrified sandstone. … After traveling several miles, we saw an opening beneath us which looked like a valley, and descending the mountain, which was very steep and high, reached a small stream flowing northeasterly [Moose Creek], just about dark, and camped where there was plenty of grass, wood, and water. In the morning (6th), we descended the stream for about five miles, and to the great surprise of us all, came to the bank of a large lake [Shoshone]. … The lake seemed to be about ten or twelve miles long, running northwest and southeast, and to be surrounded by low and thickly wooded hills which came down to the water's edge. There was a point projecting into the lake on the west side, which hid a large part of the lake from us, although we did not know it them. On the next day (7th), we went up the eastern side, near the water, passing through scrubby pines, without underbrush. There were many game trails made by the wood buffalo, whose tracks appeared numerous and fresh. We did not see any, and finally, at noon, stopped on a small prairie, for dinner. In the evening we left the lake altogether, and took a northerly course, hoping to cross the divide to some other stream. Our course lay through timber, and over and around fallen logs, but the ground, though undulating, was not rocky, and we found many game trails leading in our direction. Whenever we could obtain a glimpse of the outside world, we could see high ranges of mountains on every side. We kept on till late, without finding any place to camp, but just at dark arrived at a small dry prairie, where we camped. There was a damp place in the center, where, by digging about three feet, we soon obtained water for both ourselves and animals…"

Walter De Lacy

1871 picture of Mirror Lake and Mirror Plateau

While he enjoyed the scenery in the forests around him, De Lacy would be more interested by what was yet to come. He continued, "On the 9th, we continued our journey, and after traveling three miles, descended the mountain side into an open country. In another mile we reached the head of a small stream, the water of which was hot, and soon entered a valley or basin, through which the stream meandered, and which was occupied on every side by hot springs. They were so thick and close that we had to dismount and lead our horses, winding in and out between them as we best could. The ground sounded hollow beneath our feet, and we were in great fear of breaking through, and proceeded with great caution. The water of these springs was intensely hot, of a beautiful utramarine blue, some boiling up in the middle, and many of them of very large size, being at least twenty feet in diameter and as deep. There were hundreds of these springs, and in the distance we could see-and hear others, which would eject a column of steam with a loud noise. These were probably geysers, and the boys called them 'steamboat springs.' No one in the company had ever seen or heard of anything like this region, and we were all delighted with what we saw. This was what was afterward called the 'Lower Geyser Basin' of the Madison, by Prof. [Ferdinand Vandeveer] Hayden. We thus went on for several miles, stopping occasionally to admire the beauty, variety, and grandeur of the sight, and at length came to a large stream flowing northerly, near the banks of which were scattering hot springs, and some of which had been hot once, but had now cooled apparently, the water being tepid and muddy, with a strong smell of sulphur."

Hayden

Accompanying De Lacy on his trip was John Davis, who returned to the area the following year and later wrote an article about his journey for the *Courier-Journal* out of Louisville, Kentucky. He recalled, "We came into the park just above the lake, and immediately found ourselves in the midst of the wonders of this enchanted land. The boiling springs and geysers were all around us, and, accustomed as we were to the marvels of Western scenery, we hardly knew what to think of the phenomena. ... I went down the bank, and in short time came to the Upper Falls. The full grandeur of the scene did not burst on me at once. Men who have engaged in a hand-to-hand struggle for a frontier existence lose sentiment after a few years; but when I realized the stupendous leap of water, I could not help being impressed. I stood gazing at it for a long time, and I remember estimating the height of the falls at only about 200 feet."

Hans Jorn Storgaard Andersen's picture of the Upper Falls

As more and more of the West opened up, a number of churches began to send missionaries to the area, one of whom was Father Francis Xavier Kuppens, a Belgian Jesuit. He explained how he ended up around Yellowstone, "About the years 1865-66 I was stationed at the old Mission of St. Peter's on the Missouri River near the mouth of Sun River. ... In the spring with a small party of Indians hunting buffalo, I persuaded a few young men to show me the wonderland of which they had talked so much. Thus I got my first sight of the Yellowstone. I shall not attempt to describe it, that has been done by many abler pens than mine; but you may be sure that before leaving I saw the chief attraction,—the Grand Canyon, hot and cold geysers, variegated layers of rock, the Fire Hole, etc. I was very much impressed with the wild grandeur of the scenery, and on my return gave an account of it to Fathers Ravalli and Imoda, then stationed at the old Mission of St. Peter's."

The Grand Canyon of Yellowstone

Soon, it had become trendy for serious hunters to make a trip to the Yellowstone area. During the late 1860s, a newspaper in Virginia City announced, "The expedition to the Yellowstone country mentioned a short time since, is now organized, and it is the purpose of the party to start from the camp on Shield's river in about two weeks. The expedition will be gone some three weeks and will go up the river as far as Yellowstone Lake. As a number of gentlemen have expressed a desire to join the party, we refer those in Helena to Gen. Thoroughman who will be at that city on Monday, and will give all desired information. Parties here, who have the leisure to make this fascinating jaunt can ascertain particulars from Judge Hosmer or T. C. Everts."

A few months later, David Weaver, who had been mining in the region, reported on the exploits of the group, which was called the Bear Gulch Stampeders: "A portion of the Bear Gulch stampeders have returned. They have been to the Lake at the head of Yellowstone and report the greatest wonder of the age. For eight days they traveled through a volcanic country emitting blue flames, living streams of molten brimstone, and almost every variety of minerals known to chemists. The appearance of the country was smooth and rolling, with long level plains intervening. On the summits of these rolling mounds were craters from four to eight feet in diameter; and everywhere upon the level plains, dotting it like prairie dog holes, were smaller ones, from four to six inches and upwards. The steam and blaze was constantly discharging from these subterranean channels in regular evolutions or exhaustions, like the boilers of our steamboats, and gave the same roaring, whistling sound. As far as the eye could trace, this motion was observed. They were fearful to ascend to the craters lest the thin crust should give way and swallow them. Mr. Hubbel, (one of the party,) who has visited this region before, ventured to approach one of the smaller ones. As he neared its mouth his feet broke through and the blue flame and smoke gushed forth, enveloping him. Dropping upon his body, he crawled to within a couple of feet of the crater and saw that the crust around its edge was like a thin wafer. Lighting a match he extended it to the mouth and instantly it was on fire. The hollow ground resounded beneath their feet as they travelled on, and every moment it seemed liable to break through and bury them in its fiery vaults. The atmosphere was intensely suffocating, and they report that life could not long be sustained there. Not a living thing, bird or beast, was seen in the vicinity."

One of the best records about Yellowstone made during this period came from Bart Henderson, who kept a careful journal during his visit there in the fall of 1867. He wrote of his first view of the Upper Fall, "I was very much surprised to see the water disappear from sight. I walked out on a rock & made two steps at the same time, one forward, the other backward, for I had unawares as it were, looked down into the depths or bowels of the earth, into which the Yellow plunged as if to cool the infernal region that lay under all this wonderful country of lava & boiling springs. The water fell several feet, struck a reef of rock that projected further than the main rock above. This reef caused the water to fall the remainder of the way in spray. We judged the falls to be 80 or 90 feet high, perhaps higher."

Daniel Mayer's picture of Upper Fall

Chapter 4: These Greatest Falls

"On September 21st, a pleasant ride of eighteen miles over an undulating country brought us to the great cañon, two miles below the falls; but there being no grass convenient, we passed on up the river to a point half a mile above the upper falls, and camped on a narrow flat, close to the river bank. We spent the next day at the falls—a day that was a succession of surprises....
Above our camp the river is about one hundred and fifty yards wide, and glides smoothly along between gently-sloping banks; but just below, the hills crowd in on either side, forcing the water into a narrow channel, through which it hurries with increasing speed, until, rushing through a chute sixty feet wide, it falls in an unbroken sheet over a precipice one hundred and fifteen feet in height. It widens out again, flows with steady course for half a mile between steep timbered bluffs four hundred feet high, and again narrowing in till it is not more than seventy-five feet wide, it makes the final fearful leap of three hundred and fifty feet." - Charles Cook

By 1867, a movement had begun, though at that time only a small one, to have Yellowstone declared a national beauty spot. However, before any serious work could be done to protect the park, more had to happen that would illuminate its many wonders. Thus, the late 1860s and early 1870s saw a flurry of exploration in the area. In 1867, an article in *Frontier Index* informed readers, "Two main forks of the Yellowstone—one heading opposite Wind and Green rivers, and the other opposite Henry's Fork of Snake river, in the same vicinity that the Madison and Gallatin rise—empty into the big lake which has for its outlet the Yellowstone river, and just below the lake the whole river falls over the face of a mountain thousands of feet, the spray rising several hundred. A pebble was timed by a watch in dropping from an overhanging crag of one perpendicular fall, and is said to have required eleven and a half seconds to strike the river below. That beat Niagara Falls all 'hollow'. The river at these greatest falls is represented to be half as large as the Missouri at Omaha, and as clear as crystal. The great lake, like all others in these mountains, is thick with salmon trout of from five to forty pounds weight, and where the milky boiling mineral waters from the star bolt geysers intermingle with the pure, clear water from the running streams, elegant fish can be forked up by the boat load. A few years more and the U.P. Railroad will bring thousands of pleasure-seekers, sight-seers, and invalids from every part of the globe, to see this land of surpassing wonders." - *Frontier Index,* 1867

Similarly, in the summer of 1869, the *Helena Herald* reported, "A letter from Fort Ellis, dated the 19th, says that an expedition is organizing, composed of soldiers and citizens, and will start for the upper waters of the Yellowstone the latter part of August, and will hunt and explore a month or so. Among the places of note which they will visit, are the Falls, Coulter's Hell and Lake, and the Mysterious Mounds. The expedition is regarded as a very important one, and the result of their explorations will be looked forward to with unusual interest."

While that particular expedition did not occur, it inspired others, as explorer William Peterson later explained: "Myself and two friends—Charley Cook and D. E. Folsom who worked for the same company at Diamond that I did—after having made a trip to Helena to join the big party and finding out that they were not going to go, decided to go ourselves. It happened this way: When we got back from Helena, Cook says, 'If I could get one man to go with me, I'd go anyway.' I spoke up and said, 'Well, Charley, I guess I can go as far as you can,' and Folsom says, 'Well, I can go as far as both of ye's,' and the next thing it was, 'Shall we go?' and then, 'When shall we start?' We decided to go and started next day…"

Cook and Peterson

Folsom

As it turned out, Cook ended up writing one of the definitive accounts of the area, and one that would lead very quickly to its designation as a national park at that. In 1869, he sold his story to the *Western Monthly Magazine* in Chicago, Illinois for $18.00. An article credited to both Cook and Folsom appeared in 1870: "We pushed on up the valley, following the general course of the river as well as we could, but frequently making short detours through the foot-hills, to avoid the deep ravines and places where the hills terminated abruptly at the water's edge. ... we travelled over a high rolling table-land, diversified by sparkling lakes, picturesque rocks, and beautiful groves of timber. Two or three miles to our left, we could see the deep gorge which the river, flowing westward, had cut through the mountains. The river soon after resumed its northern course; and from this point to the falls, a distance of twenty-five or thirty miles, it is believed to flow through one continuous cañon, through which no one has ever been able to pass. At this point we left the main river, intending to follow up the east branch for one day, then to turn in a southwest course and endeavor to strike the river again near the falls. After going a short distance, we encountered a cañon about three miles in length, and while passing around it we caught a glimpse of scenery so grand and striking that we decided to stop for a day or two and give it a more extended examination."

One of the things that makes Yellowstone so stunning is the constant juxtaposition of heights and depths. Cook noted, "We picked our way to a timbered point about mid-way of the cañon, and found ourselves upon the verge of an overhanging cliff at least seven hundred feet in height. The opposite bluff was about on a level with the place where we were standing; and it maintained this height for a mile up the river, but gradually sloped away toward the foot of the cañon. The upper half presented an unbroken face, with here and there a re-entering angle, but everywhere maintained its perpendicularity; the lower half was composed of the debris that had fallen from the wall. But the most singular feature was the formation of the perpendicular wall. At the top, there was a stratum of basalt, from thirty to forty feet thick, standing in hexagonal columns; beneath that, a bed of conglomerate eighty feet thick, composed of washed gravel and boulders; then another stratum of columnar basalt of about half the thickness of the first; and lastly what appeared to be a bed of coarse sandstone. A short distance above us, rising from the bed of the river, stood a monument or pyramid of conglomerate, circular in form, which we estimated to be forty feet in diameter at the base, and three hundred feet high, diminishing in size in a true taper to its top, which was not more than three feet across. It was so slender that it looked as if one man could topple it over."

The Yellowstone River, from which the region and later the park took its name, is one of the most beautiful and certainly the most interesting in the west, as others have already observed. Cook himself added, "We could see the river for nearly the whole distance through the cañon dashing over some miniature cataract, now fretting against huge boulders that seemed to have been hurled by some giant hand to stay its progress, and anon circling in quiet eddies beneath the dark shadows of some projecting rock. The water was so transparent that we could see the bottom from where we were standing, and it had that peculiar liquid emerald tinge so characteristic of our mountain streams. Half a mile down the river, and near the foot of the bluff, was a chalky-looking bank, from which steam and smoke were rising; and on repairing to the spot, we found a vast number of hot sulphur springs. The steam was issuing from every crevice and hole in the rocks; and, being highly impregnated with sulphur, it threw off sulphureted hydrogen, making a stench that was very unpleasant. All the crevices were lined with beautiful crystals of sulphur, as delicate as frost-work. At some former period, not far distant, there must have been a volcanic eruption here. Much of the scoria and ashes which were then thrown out has been carried off by the river, but enough still remains to form a bar, seventy-five or a hundred feet in depth. Smoke was still issuing from the rocks in one place, from which a considerable amount of lava had been discharged within a few days or weeks at farthest. While we were standing by, several gallons of a black liquid ran down and hardened upon the rocks; we broke some of this off and brought it away, and it proved to be sulphur, pure enough to burn readily when ignited."

Mike Cline's picture of Yellowstone River and Black Canyon

As Cook quickly learned, there is much more to Yellowstone than the geysers. "Resuming our journey, we soon saw the serrated peaks of the Big Horn Range glistening like burnished silver in the sunlight, and, over-towering them in the dim distance, the Wind River Mountains seemed to blend with the few fleecy clouds that skirted their tops; while in the opposite direction, in contrast to the barren snow-capped peaks behind us, as far as the eye could reach, mountain and valley were covered with timber, whose dark green foliage deepened in hue as it receded, till it terminated at the horizon in a boundless black forest. Taking our bearings as well as we could, we shaped our course in the direction in which we supposed the falls to be. The next day (September 20th), we came to a gentle declivity at the head of a shallow ravine, from which steam rose in a hundred columns and united in a cloud so dense as to obscure the sun. In some places it spurted from the rocks in jets not larger than a pipe-stem; in others it curled gracefully up from the surface of boiling pools from five to fifteen feet in diameter. In some springs the water was clear and transparent; others contained so much sulphur that they looked like pots of boiling yellow paint. One of the largest was as black as ink. Near this was a fissure in the rocks, several rods long and two feet across in the widest place at the surface, but enlarging as it descended. We could not see down to any great depth, on account of the steam but the ground echoed beneath our tread with a hollow sound, and we could hear the waters surging below, sending up a dull, resonant roar like the break of the ocean surf into a cave. At these springs but little water was discharged at the surface, it seeming to pass off by some subterranean passage. About half a mile down the ravine, the springs broke out again. Here they were in groups, spreading out over several acres of ground."

The Bighorn Mountains

One of the most unique features of Yellowstone is the wide variety of minerals found in the park. These minerals produce many of the effects described here and elsewhere, including making the mud itself a thing of beauty. According to Cook, "One of these groups—a collection of mud springs of various colors, situated one above the other on the left slope of the ravine—we christened 'The Chemical Works.' The mud, as it was discharged from the lower side, gave each spring the form of a basin or pool. At the bottom of the slope was a vat, ten by thirty feet, where all the ingredients from the springs above were united in a greenish-yellow compound of the consistency of white lead. Three miles further on we found more hot springs along the sides of a deep ravine, at the bottom of which flowed a creek twenty feet wide. Near the bank of the creek, through an aperture four inches in diameter, a column of steam rushed with a deafening roar, with such force that it maintained its size for forty feet in the air, then spread out and rolled away in a great cloud toward the heavens. We found here inexhaustible beds of sulphur and saltpeter.

Alum was also abundant; a small pond in the vicinity, some three hundred yards long and half as wide, contained as much alum as it could hold in solution, and the mud along the shore was white with the same substance, crystallized by evaporation."

In some places, the water itself put on a show, as Cook described. "The ragged edges of the precipice tear the water into a thousand streams—all united together, and yet apparently separate,—changing it to the appearance of molten silver; the outer ones decrease in size as they increase in velocity, curl outward, and break into mist long before they reach the bottom. This cloud of mist conceals the river for two hundred yards, but it dashes out from beneath the rainbow-arch that spans the chasm, and thence, rushing over a succession of rapids and cascades, it vanishes at last, where a sudden turn of the river seems to bring the two walls of the cañon together. Below the falls, the hills gradually increase in height for two miles, where they assume the proportions of mountains. Here the cañon is at least fifteen hundred feet deep, with an average width of twice that distance at the top. For one-third of the distance downwards the sides are perpendicular,—from thence running down to the river in steep ridges crowned by rocks of the most grotesque form and color; and it required no stretch of the imagination to picture fortresses, castles, watch-towers, and other ancient structures, of every conceivable shape. In several places near the bottom, steam issued from the rocks; and, judging from the indications, there were at some former period hot springs or steam-jets of immense size all along the wall."

Soon, Cook and his party came face-to-face with Yellowstone's most dramatic features: "The next day we resumed our journey, traversing the northern slope of a high plateau between the Yellowstone and Snake Rivers. Unlike the dashing mountain—stream we had thus far followed, the Yellowstone was in this part of its course wide and deep, flowing with a gentle current along the foot of low hills, or meandering in graceful curves through broad and grassy meadows. Some twelve miles from the falls we came to a collection of hot springs that deserve more than a passing notice. These, like the most we saw, were situated upon a hillside; and as we approached them we could see the steam rising in puffs at regular intervals of fifteen or twenty seconds, accompanied by dull explosions which could be heard half a mile away, sounding like the discharge of a blast underground. These explosions came from a large cave that ran back under the hill, from which mud had been discharged in such quantities as to form a heavy embankment twenty feet higher than the floor of the cave, which prevented the mud from flowing off; but the escaping steam had kept a hole, some twenty feet in diameter, open up through the mud in front of the entrance to the cave. The cave seemed nearly filled with mud, and the steam rushed out with such volume and force as to lift the whole mass up against the roof and dash it out into the open space in front; and then, as the cloud of steam lifted, we could see the mud settling back in turbid waves into the cavern again. Three hundred yards from the mud-cave was another that discharged pure water; the entrance to it was in the form of a perfect arch, seven feet in height and five in width. A short distance below these caves were several large sulphur springs, the most remarkable of which was a shallow pool seventy-five feet in diameter, in which clear water on one side and yellow mud on the other were gently boiling without mingling."

As if Yellowstone's natural beauty wasn't enough considering the mountains, falls, rivers, and geysers, Cook was blown away the most by Yellowstone Lake. "September 24th we arrived at Yellowstone Lake, about twenty miles from the falls. The main body of this beautiful sheet of water is ten miles wide from east to west, and sixteen miles long from north to south; but at the south end it puts out two arms, one to the southeast and the other to the southwest, making the entire length of the lake about thirty miles. Its shores—whether gently sloping mountains, bold promontories, low necks, or level prairies—are everywhere covered with timber. The lake has three small islands, which are also heavily timbered. The outlet is at the northwest extremity. The lake abounds with trout, and the shallow water in its coves affords feeding ground for thousands of wild ducks, geese, pelicans, and swans. We ascended to the head of the lake, and remained in its vicinity for several days, resting ourselves and our horses, and viewing the many objects of interest and wonder. Among these were springs differing from any we had previously seen. They were situated along the shore for a distance of two miles, extending back from it about five hundred yards and into the lake perhaps as many feet. The ground in many places gradually sloped down to the water's edge, while in others the white chalky cliffs rose fifteen feet high—the waves having worn the rock away at the base, leaving the upper portion projecting over in some places twenty feet. There were several hundred springs here, varying in size from miniature fountains to pools or wells seventy-five feet in diameter and of great depth; the water had a pale violet tinge, and was very clear, enabling us to discern small objects fifty or sixty feet below the surface. In some of these, vast openings led off at the side; and as the slanting rays of the sun lit up these deep caverns, we could see the rocks hanging from their roofs, their water-worn sides and rocky floors, almost as plainly as if we had been traversing their silent chambers."

1871 pictures of Yellowstone Lake

The springs were particularly delightful to the travel-weary men, as Cook recalled: "These springs were intermittent, flowing or boiling at irregular intervals. The greater portion of them were perfectly quiet while we were there, although nearly all gave unmistakable evidence of frequent activity. Some of them would quietly settle for ten feet, while another would as quietly rise until it overflowed its banks, and send a torrent of hot water sweeping down to the lake. At the same time, one near at hand would send up a sparkling jet of water ten or twelve feet high, which would fall back into its basin, and then perhaps instantly stop boiling and quietly settle into the earth, or suddenly rise and discharge its waters in every direction over the rim; while another, as if wishing to attract our wondering gaze, would throw up a cone six feet in diameter and eight feet high, with a loud roar. These changes, each one of which would possess some new feature, were constantly going on; sometimes they would occur within the space of a few minutes, and again hours would elapse before any change could be noted. At the water's edge, along the lake shore, there were several mounds of solid stone, on the top of each of which was a small basin with a perforated bottom; these also overflowed at times, and the hot water trickled down on every side. Thus, by the slow process of precipitation, through the countless lapse of ages, these stone monuments have been formed. A small cluster of mud springs nearby claimed our attention. They were like hollow truncated cones and oblong mounds, three or four feet in height. These were filled with mud, resembling thick paint of the finest quality—differing in color, from pure white to the various shades of yellow, pink, red, and violet. Some of these boiling pots were less than a foot in diameter. The mud in them would slowly rise and fall as the bubbles of escaping steam, following one after the other, would burst upon the surface. During the afternoon, they threw mud to the height of fifteen feet for a few minutes, and then settled back to their former quietude."

Just when Cook thought he had seen all that the region had to offer, he came across one last surprise:

"As we were about departing on our homeward trip, we ascended the summit of a neighboring hill, and took a final look at Yellowstone Lake. Nestled among the forest-crowned hills which bounded our vision, lay this inland sea, its crystal waves dancing and sparkling in the sunlight, as if laughing with joy for their wild freedom. It is a scene of transcendent beauty, which has been viewed by but few white men; and we felt glad to have looked upon it before its primeval solitude should be broken by the crowds of pleasure-seekers which at no distant day will throng its shores. [On] September 29th, we took up our march for home. Our plan was to cross the range in a northwesterly direction, find the Madison River, and follow it down to civilization. Twelve miles brought us to a small triangular-shaped lake, about eight miles long, deeply set among the hills. We kept on in a northwesterly direction, as near as the rugged nature of the country would permit; and on the third day (October 1st) came to a small irregularly shaped valley, some six miles across in the widest place, from every part of which great clouds of steam arose. From descriptions which we had had of this valley, from persons who had previously visited it, we recognized it as the place known as 'Burnt Hole,' or 'Death Valley.' The Madison River flows through it, and from the general contour of the country we knew that it headed in the lake which we passed two days ago, only twelve miles from the Yellowstone."

"We descended into the valley, and found that the springs had the same general characteristics as those I have already described, although some of them were much larger and discharged a vast amount of water. One of them, at a little distance, attracted our attention by the immense amount of steam it threw off; and upon approaching it we found it to be an intermittent geyser in active operation. The hole through which the water was discharged was ten feet in diameter, and was situated in the center of a large circular shallow basin, into which the water fell. There was a stiff breeze blowing at the time, and by going to the windward side and carefully picking our way over convenient stones, we were enabled to reach the edge of the hole. At that moment the escaping steam was causing the water to boil up in a fountain five or six feet high. It stopped in an instant, and commenced settling down—twenty, thirty, forty feet—until we concluded that the bottom had fallen out; but the next instant, without any warning, it came rushing up and shot into the air at least eighty feet, causing us to stampede for higher ground. It continued to spout at intervals of a few minutes, for some time; but finally subsided, and was quiet during the remainder of the time we stayed in the vicinity. We followed up the Madison five miles, and there found the most gigantic hot springs we had seen. They were situated along the river bank, and discharged so much hot water that the river was blood-warm a quarter of a mile below. One of the springs was two hundred and fifty feet in diameter, and had every indication of spouting powerfully at times. The waters from the hot springs in this valley, if united, would form a large stream; and they increase the size of the river nearly one-half."

Finally, Cook concluded his account: "Leaving this remarkable valley, we followed the course of the Madison—sometimes through level valleys, and sometimes through deep cuts in mountain ranges,—and on the fourth of October emerged from a cañon, ten miles long and with high and precipitous mountain sides, to find the broad valley of the Lower Madison spread out before us. Here we could recognize familiar landmarks in some of the mountain peaks around Virginia City. From this point we completed our journey by easy stages, and arrived at home on the evening of the eleventh."

Chapter 5: A Park Worthy of the Great Republic

"Such, in brief, has been the origin and progress of this project now about to receive a definite and permanent shape in the establishment of a National Park. It will be a park worthy of the Great Republic. If it contains the proportions set forth in Clagett's bill, it will embrace about 2,500 square miles, and include the great canyon, the Falls and Lake of the Yellowstone, with a score of other magnificent lakes, the great geyser basin of the Madison, and thousands of mineral and boiling springs. Should the whole surface of the earth be gleaned, another spot of equal dimensions could not be found that contains on such a magnificent scale one-half the attractions here grouped together."- A newspaper article in the early 1870s

The Cook-Folsom expedition yield an excellent and inspiring article that provided extensive fuel for the pro-park movement, and it also provided both the government and the general public with new and improved maps of the region. Most of all, it persuaded others in the country to visit the area and see the great wonders for themselves. In 1871, A. B. Nettleton of the Jay Cooke & Co., Bankers, Financial Agents, Northern Pacific Railroad Company, wrote to Professor Hayden, who had returned to Washington D.C.: "Judge [William] Kelley has made a suggestion which strikes me as being an excellent one, viz.: Let Congress pass a bill reserving the Great Geyser Basin as a public park forever—just as it has reserved that far inferior wonder the Yosemite Valley and big trees. If you approve this would such a recommendation be appropriate in your official report?" Hayden agreed with this suggestion and word got out that Yellowstone might soon become a protected area.

At this point, others in the railroad business became interested given the vast amount of space and potential property rights. Jay Cooke wrote to an engineer at Northern Pacific with concern: "It is proposed by Mr. Hayden in his report to Congress that the Geyser region around Yellowstone Lake shall be set apart by government as a reservation as park, similar to that of the Great Trees & other reservations in California. Would this conflict with our land grant, or interfere with us in any way? Please give me your views on this subject. It is important to do something speedily, or squatters & claimants will go in there, and we can probably deal much better with the government in any improvements we may desire to make for the benefit of our pleasure travel than with individuals."

As it turned out, the area being set aside for the park was outside Northern Pacific's planned route, but this marked the first of many conflicts that would occur through the decades between conservationists and big business. In Northern Pacific's case, the company quickly became an avid supporter of the project, no doubt in part because of the number of tourists it would bring to the region.

A 1921 Union Pacific advertisement

Others in the area were also enthusiastic and anxious to benefit from such a decision. One Montana newspaper proclaimed, "The great falls and wonderful geysers of the Upper Yellowstone, now receiving universal attention, should be forever set apart as a resort for the scientific students and pleasure seekers of the world; and for the convenience of protective local legislation, they should be included within the boundaries of Montana Territory. They are situated beyond our lines and within the jurisdiction of Wyoming; but are practically a barren heritage to our sister Territory, for the reason that rugged, and in winter altogether impassable, mountains separate them from her capital and chief cities. . . . From this side, the Great Falls may be reached and all the surrounding wonders and curiosities explored at any month of the year. . . . As nearly the entire length of the Yellowstone River is in Montana, it is eminently right and proper that its fountains should also be. Congress should donate the extreme Upper Yellowstone, with its mighty cataracts and other marvels to this Territory, to be set apart and protected under appropriate local legislation, as a resort for pleasure and scientific investigation forever. Has not Montana thrown as much gold into the commercial channels of trade and commerce as California had, up to the time that the valley of the Yosemite was thus granted to her by the General Government? And we are satisfied our neighbors of Wyoming would be too reasonable and generous to object to the grant, in the face of the fact that natural circumstances render the prize utterly worthless to them. We understand our wide-awake Delegate will introduce a bill, the present session, asking for appointment of a commission to readjust our boundary, so as to include the Upper Yellowstone, and we suggest to Messrs. Beck and Vivion, our representatives in the Legislature, that a co-operative memorial would be very proper."

To be fair, there was precedent for Montana's request, because the federal government had yet to involve itself in any sort of national park programs to that point. In fact, it had just a few years earlier turned the Yosemite Valley over to California for management and protection. On the other hand, whereas all of Yosemite is in California, much of Yellowstone was in Wyoming, and it also extends into Idaho.

Initially, there was little interest on the part of those living in the area around Yellowstone to see it set aside for any purpose. However, as the *Deer Lodge New North-West* out of Montana observed, "to it will come in the coming years thousands from every quarter of the globe, to look with awe upon its amazing phenomena, and with pen, pencil, tongue and camera publish its marvels to the enlightened realms. Let this, too, be set apart by Congress as a domain retained unto all mankind, (Indians not taxed, excepted), and let it be esto perpetua."

Likewise, the *Virginia City Daily Territorial Enterprise* in Nevada opined, "The Hon. N. P. Langford of Montana, the leader [sic] of the famous Yellowstone Expedition of 1870, and several scientific and literary gentlemen, is engaged in an effort to have the Yellowstone region declared a National Park. The district, of which some features have been described in Scribner's Monthly, is said to be un-adapted to agriculture, mining or manufacturing purposes, and it is proposed to have its magnificent scenery, hot springs, geysers and cataracts forever dedicated to public uses as a grand national reservation. Congress is to be petitioned to this effect."

Langford

Finally, in 1872, a bill came before the United States Congress saying in part that Yellowstone "is hereby reserved and withdrawn from settlement, occupancy, or sale. . . and dedicated and set apart as a public park or pleasuring-ground for the benefit and enjoyment of the people.... The Secretary may, in his discretion, grant leases for building purposes for terms not exceeding 10 years, of small parcels of ground.... All of the proceeds of said leases, and all other revenues that may be derived from any source connected with said park, to be expended under his direction in the management of the same, and the construction of roads and bridle paths therein."

In reporting on this, one Helena newspaper reported, "We have not seen the text of this particular bill, and cannot say if it is identical with that introduced in the House by our Delegate, but presume it to be essentially the same; and judging from the readiness with which the idea has been taken up, put into shape, and passed the Senate, there can be little doubt that very soon it will receive the sanction of the necessary parties and become a law. In fact, since the idea was first conceived by the party of gentlemen from this city, who visited this region of wonders in the summer of 1869 [sic], and gave to the world the first reliable reports concerning its marvelous wealth of natural curiosities, the project has gained ground with surprising rapidity. The letters of Mr. Hedges, first published in the HERALD, the lectures of Mr. Langford, the articles of Mr. Trumbull, and later still, the story of [the] peril and adventure of Mr. Everts, all of the same party, were widely circulated by the press of the country, and not merely excited a passing curiosity, but created a living, general interest that has since received strength and larger proportions by the publication of Lieutenant Doane's official report to the War Department of the same expedition; followed, as it was, by the expedition of Professor Hayden, during the last summer, under the patronage of the Smithsonian Institution, with its fully appointed corps of scientific gentlemen and distinguished artists, whose reports have more than confirmed all descriptions of the Washburn party. ... Without a doubt the Northern Pacific Railroad will have a branch track penetrating this Plutonian region, and few seasons will pass before excursion trains will daily be sweeping into this great park thousands of the curious from all parts of the world."

Of course, not everyone who knew about the project was enthusiastic. Those who had already settled on the land were particularly unhappy, and they had their fair share of supporters. The *Rocky Mountain Weekly Gazette* in Helena complained, "As for ourselves we regard the project with little favor, unless Congress will go still further and make appropriations to open carriage roads through, and hostels in, the reserved district, so that ordinary humanity can get into it without having to ride on the "Hurricane deck" of a mule…. Already private enterprise was taking measures to render the country accessible to such tourists as are not strong enough to endure the fatigues of a regular exploring expedition….If Congress sets off that scope of country as proposed, all these private enterprises will immediately cease, and as it is not at all likely that the Government will make any appropriations to open roads or hostelries, the country will be remanded into a wilderness and rendered inaccessible to the great mass of travelers and tourists for many years to come…. We are opposed to any scheme which will have a tendency to remand it into perpetual solitude, by shutting out private enterprise and by preventing individual energy from opening the country to the general traveling public."

Nevertheless, the bill passed the Congress and was soon signed into law by President Grant. In celebrating the act, the *Helena Daily Herald* reported, "Our dispatches announce the passage in the House of the Senate bill setting apart the Upper Yellowstone Valley for the purposes of a National Park. The importance to Montana of this Congressional enactment cannot be too highly estimated. It will redound to the untold good of this Territory, inasmuch as a measure of this character is well calculated to direct the world's attention to a very important section of country that to the present time has passed largely unnoticed. It will be the means of centering on Montana the attention of thousands heretofore comparatively uninformed of a Territory abounding in such resources of mines and of agriculture and of wonderland as we can boast, spread everywhere about us."

Back east, the *New York Times* also praised the decision: "It is a satisfaction to know that the Yellowstone Park bill has passed the House. Our readers have been made well acquainted with the beautiful and astonishing features of a region unlike any other in the world; and will approve the policy by which, while the title is still vested in the United States, provision has been made to retain it perpetually for the nation. The Yosemite Valley was similarly appropriated to public use some years back, and that magnificent spot was thus saved from possible defacement or other unseemly treatment that might have attended its remaining in private hands.... The new National Park lies in two Territories, Montana and Wyoming, but the jurisdiction of the soil, by the passage of the bill, remains forever with the Federal Government. In this respect the position of the Yellowstone Park differs from that of the Yosemite; since the latter was granted by Government to the State of California on certain conditions one of which excludes the local control of the United States; while the former will always be within that control. Perhaps, no scenery in the world surpasses for sublimity that of the Yellowstone Valley; and certainly no region anywhere is so rich, in the same space, in wonderful natural curiosities. In addition to this, from the height of the land, and the salubrity of the atmosphere, physicians are of opinion that the Yellowstone Park will become a valuable resort for certain classes of invalids; and in all probability it will soon appear that the mineral springs, with which the place abounds, possess various curative powers. It is far from unlikely that the park may become in a few years the Baden or Homburg of America, and that strangers may flock thither from all parts of the world to drink the waters, and gaze on picturesque splendors only to be seen in the heart of the American Continent."

Another Eastern newspaper happily predicted, "It is the general principle which is chiefly commendable in the act of Congress setting aside the Yellowstone region as a national park. It will help confirm the national possession of the Yosemite, and may in time lead us to rescue Niagara from its present degrading surroundings. That the park will not very soon be accessible to the public needs no demonstration."

Meanwhile, back in Bozeman, Montana, a group of tourists were gathering together to become the first of millions of visitors who would tour the park over the next dozen decades. As the *New York Herald* put it, "Why should we go to Switzerland to see mountains, or to Iceland for geysers? Thirty years ago the attraction of America to the foreign mind was Niagara Falls. Now we have attractions which diminish Niagara into an ordinary exhibition. The Yo Semite, which the nation has made a park, the Rocky mountains and their singular parks, the canyons of the

Colorado, the Dalles of the Columbia, the giant trees, the lake country of Minnesota, the country of the Yellowstone, with their beauty, their splendor, their extraordinary and sometimes terrible manifestations of nature, form a series of attractions possessed by no other nation in the world."

A 1938 advertisement for Yellowstone

A 1941 picture of Old Faithful

Upper Terraces of Mammoth Hot Springs

Bibliography

Cook, Charles W. (July 1870). "The Valley of the Upper Yellowstone". *Western Monthly Magazine* IV: 60–67.

Cook, Charles W.; Folsom, Dave E.; Peterson, William (1965). Haines, Aubrey L., ed. *The Valley of the Upper Yellowstone-An Exploration of the Headwaters of the Yellowstone River in the Year 1869*. Norman, OK: University of Oklahoma Press.

Haines, Aubrey L. (1977). *The Yellowstone Story-A History of Our First National Park*. Yellowstone National Park, WY: Yellowstone Library and Museum Association.

Hayden, F. V. (1880). The Great West: Its Attractions and Resources, Containing a Popular Description of the Marvelous Scenery, Physical Geography, Fossils and Glaciers of the Wonderful Region, And the Recent Explorations of the Yellowstone Park,

Chittenden, Hiram Martin (1918). *The Yellowstone Park-Historical and Descriptive*. Cincinnati, Ohio: Stewart and Kidd Company Publishers.

Henderson, G. L. (1891). *Yellowstone National Park, Past, Present and Future*. Washington, D.C.: Gibson Brothers.

Langford, Nathaniel P. (1904). "Preface to The Folsom Cook Exploration of the Upper Yellowstone, 1869 (1894)". *Contributions to the Historical Society of Montana* V: 354–55.

Merrill, Marlene Deahl, ed. (1999). *Yellowstone and the Great West-Journals, Letters and Images from the 1871 Hayden Expedition*. Lincoln, NE: University of Nebraska Press.

Schullery, Paul; Whittlesey, Lee (2003). *Myth and History in the Creation of Yellowstone National Park*. Lincoln, NE: University of Nebraska Press.

Schwatka, Frederick; Hyde, John (1886). *Through Wonderland with Lieutenant Schwatka*. St. Paul, MN: Northern Pacific Railroad.

Topping, E. S. (1888). *The Chronicles of the Yellowstone*. St Paul, MN: Pioneer Press Co.[4]

Vinton, Stallo (1926). *John Colter-Discoverer of Yellowstone Park*. New York: Edward Iberstadt.

Printed in Poland
by Amazon Fulfillment
Poland Sp. z o.o., Wrocław